Another First Poetry Book

compiled by
John Foster

Oxford University Press

Oxford University Press, Great Clarendon Street, Oxford OX2 6DP

Oxford   New York
Athens Auckland Bangkok Bogota Buenos Aires Calcutta
Cape Town Chennai Dar es Salaam Delhi Florence
Hong Kong Istanbul Karachi Kuala Lumpur Madrid
Melbourne Mexico City Mumbai Nairobi Paris São Paulo
Singapore Taipei Tokyo Toronto Warsaw

and associated companies in
Berlin Ibadan

Oxford is a trade mark of Oxford University Press

A CIP record for this book is available from the British Library

ISBN 0 19 916228 X

Phototypeset by Tradespools Limited, Frome, Somerset
Printed in Hong Kong

Contents

Everybody Says

Everybody says
I look just like my mother.
Everybody says
I'm the image of Aunt Bee.
Everybody says
My nose is like my father's
But *I* want to look like *ME*!

Dorothy Aldis

My Dad

My Dad and I
are not at all alike.
He's tall, with darkish hair
and drives a car to work –
I'm short and fair
and ride a bike.

My Dad and I
like different food.
He loves a huge roast lamb
with gravy, peas and mash –
I'd rather have some ham
with jacket spud.

My Dad and I
are not at all the same.
I like to swim,
play football in the park;
it's always chess for him –
a very different game.

My Dad and I
are different in our ways.
I am the early bird,
up with the sun or haze –
he likes to sleep in late,
especially Saturdays.

My Dad and I
may not *appear* to match,
but when he comes to swim
or shows me chess
or takes me to the park
to play football
it's clear to me and him
that after all
we're *not* a different batch!

Judith Nicholls

8

Dad

Dad is the dancing-man,
The laughing-bear, the prickle-chin,
The tickle-fingers, jungle-roars,
Bucking bronco, rocking-horse,
The helicopter round-about
The beat-the-wind at swing-and-shout
Goal-post, scarey-ghost,
Climbing-jack, humpty-back.

But sometimes he's
A 'Go-away-please'
A snorey snarl, a sleeping slump,
A yawny mouth, a sprawly lump –
And I'm a kite without a string
Waiting for Dad to dance again.

Berlie Doherty

9

Emma Hackett's Newsbook

Last night my mum
Got really mad
And threw a jam tart
At my dad.
Dad lost his temper
Then with mother,
Threw one at her
And hit my brother.
My brother thought
It was my sister,
Threw two at her
But somehow missed her.
My sister,
She is only three,
Hurled four at him
And one at me!

I said I wouldn't
Stand for that,
Aimed one at her
And hit the cat.
The cat jumped up
Like he'd been shot,
And landed
In the baby's cot.
The baby –
Quietly sucking his thumb –
Then started howling
For my mum.
At which my mum
Got *really* mad,
And threw a Swiss roll
At my dad.

Allan Ahlberg

Where Did the Baby Go?

I cannot remember –
And neither can my Mother –
Just when it was our baby
Turned into my brother.

Julie Holder

Sister

Tell me a story!
Lend me that book!
Please, let me come in your den.
I won't mess it up,
so *please* say I can.
When? When? When?

Lend me that engine,
that truck – and your glue.
I'll give half of my old bubblegum.
You know what Dad said
about learning to share.
Give it *now,*
or I'm telling Mum!

Oh, *please* lend your bike –
I'll be careful this time.
I'll keep out of the mud
and the snow.
I could borrow your hat –
the one you've just got . . . . .
                        said my sister.

And I said

NO!

Judith Nicholls

My Sister

My sister's remarkably light,
She can float to a fabulous height.
It's a troublesome thing,
But we tie her with string,
And we use her instead of a kite.

Margaret Mahy

Ticklish

One day as I passed the bathroom door
I heard what sounded like a roar
and then a scream like a parakeet –
it was only my brother washing his feet.

Every time he takes a bath
all he can do is laugh and laugh.
He's ticklish from nose to knees;
armpits and elbows are a tease

and if he's laughing fit to burst
he's reached his toes – the very worst.
To be so ticklish is a bore –
when I hear him chuckling I'm sure

I'd rather be ticklish here and there
and not, like he is, everywhere.

Pamela Gillilan

Bubble Gum

I'm in trouble
made a bubble
peeled it off my nose

Felt a rock
inside my sock
got gum between my toes

Made another
told my brother
we could blow a pair

Give three cheers
now our ears,
are sticking to our hair.

Nina Payne

I Wish I Could Meet the Man That Knows

I wish I could meet the man that knows
Who put the fly on my daddy's nose
When my daddy was taking a nap today.
I tried to slap that fly away
So Daddy could sleep. But just as my hand
Came down to slap him the fly jumped, AND

I hit with a bang – where do you suppose? –
SMACK ON THE END OF DADDY'S
    NOSE!

"Ow!" cried Daddy, and up he jumped.
He jumped so hard that he THUMP-
    BUMPED
His head on the wall.
           Well, I tried to say,
"See, Daddy, I slapped the fly away."
And I should think he would have thanked me.
But what do you think he did? He
    SPANKED me!

"I was just trying to help!" I said.
But Daddy was looking very red.
"For trying to help, I have to thank you.
But for that smack on the nose, I'll spank
    you!"
And up in the air went his great big hand
As he said, "I hope you understand
It's my nose I'm spanking for, not the fly.
For the fly I thank you."

And that is why
I wish I could meet the man that knows
Who put the fly on my daddy's nose.
For when I find him, I want to thank him.
And as I do, I want to spank him.

John Ciardi

Granny Granny Please Comb My Hair

Granny Granny
please comb my hair
you always take your time
you always take such care

You put me to sit on a cushion
between your knees
you rub a little coconut oil
parting gentle as a breeze

Mummy Mummy
she's always in a hurry-hurry
rush
she pulls my hair
sometimes she tugs

But Granny
you have all the time in the world
and when you're finished
you always turn my head and say
'Now who's a nice girl.'

Grace Nichols

My Sparrow Gran

My Sparrow Gran
Is the singing one
Busy and tidy
And brown-bright-eyed
She chirrups and chats
She scurries and darts
She picks up the bits
That clutter her nest
And when evening comes
When all her work's done
I bring her my book
And sit on her lap
Snug in her arms
That are feather-down warm.

Berlie Doherty

Grandpa is very old

Grandpa is very old, you know;
In his ears
Bristle the hairs of many greying years;
His neck is folded with the loose, cloth skin
That hangs below the stubble of his chin;
And on his hands
The purple veins
Lie thick like worms
After the summer rains.

And when he bones me on his knee
I feel his body smile at me,
And when he hugs me with his arm
And pulls that face so scowly-grim
I feel I'm looking after him.

Gregory Harrison

20

Grandpa

Grandpa's hands are as rough as garden sacks
And as warm as pockets.
His skin is crushed paper round his eyes,
Wrapping up their secrets.

Berlie Doherty

21

In Hall

'All things bright and beautiful . . .'
How many late today?
There's mud all up the front staircase,
What is she going to say?

It's hot in here, I'm going to sneeze.
'All creatures great and small . . .'
A spider's dangling over her!
Where is it going to fall?

It might land softly in her hair –
would she feel it, d'you suppose?
Or, if it swung a little bit,
it might settle on her nose.

'All things wise and wonderful . . .'
The teachers stand in line.
It's only got an inch to go!
This may be a sign.

Oh, land on her, please land on her!
'The Lord God made them all . . .'
Then she'll forget she saw me there –
I was here, in Hall,

I wasn't late, I didn't leave
my footsteps on the stairs . . .
Oh! Spider, you must hurry up,
she's halfway through the prayers.

Spider, spider, burning bright . . .
'Three girls I want to see.
Where are you? You, and you, and . . . Oh!
What's this? Oh dear! Dear me! . . .'

A hundred eyes, eight hairy legs,
A shadow on the wall.
I wasn't there, I wasn't late.
The Lord God loves us all!

Jane Whittle

23

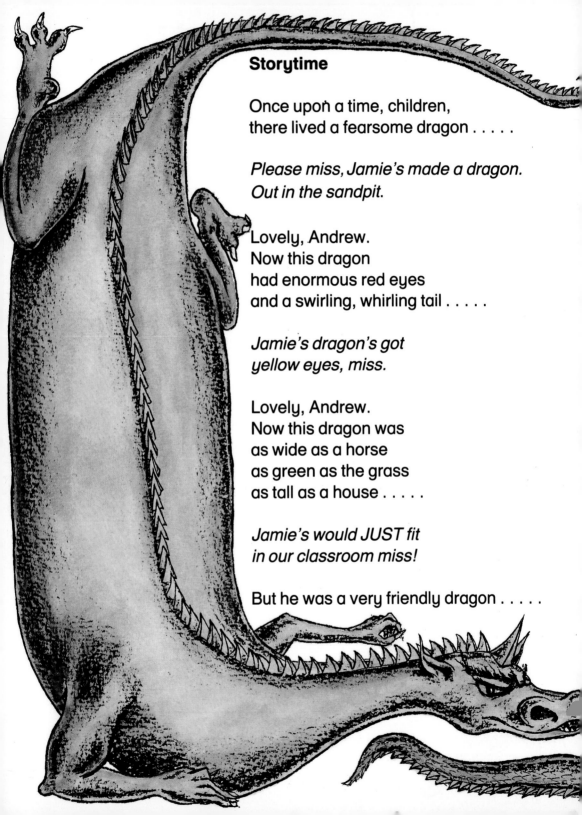

Storytime

Once upon a time, children,
there lived a fearsome dragon . . . . .

Please miss, Jamie's made a dragon.
Out in the sandpit.

Lovely, Andrew.
Now this dragon
had enormous red eyes
and a swirling, whirling tail . . . . .

Jamie's dragon's got
yellow eyes, miss.

Lovely, Andrew.
Now this dragon was
as wide as a horse
as green as the grass
as tall as a house . . . . .

Jamie's would JUST fit
in our classroom miss!

But he was a very friendly dragon . . . . .

Jamie's dragon ISN'T, miss.
He eats people, miss.
Especially TEACHERS,
Jamie said.

Very nice, Andrew!
Now one day, children,
this enormous dragon
rolled his red eye,
whirled his swirly green tail
and set off to find . . . . .

His dinner, miss!
Because he was hungry, miss!

Thank you, Andrew.
He rolled his red eye,
whirled his green tail,
and opened his wide, wide mouth
until oo oouuaaaah!

Please miss,
I did try to tell you, miss!

Judith Nicholls

25

Teacher Teacher

teacher
teacher
come here quick
Stella Brown's
been awful sick

teacher
teacher
got here late
his head got stuck
in the school front gate

teacher
teacher
I'm fed up
can't control
this hic –

      hic –

         hiccup

teacher
teacher
you're the best
when you wear
that old string vest

teacher
teacher
I'm off home
got to feed
my garden gnome

Wes Magee

Friends

I'll read with you, and play with you,
I'll sit in school all day with you,
I'll give you my best lego set,
I'll do your writing, so you'll get
A gold star, and my car I'll lend
To you 'cause you're my best, best friend.

Enemies

I'll tear your coat, I'll mangle you,
I'll grab your throat and strangle you,
I'll scribble on your reading book,
I'll throw your bag from off the hook,
I'll put a worm into your tea,
You are my worst, worst enemy.

Theresa Heine

Down by the School Gate

There goes the bell
it's half past three
and down by the school gate
you will see. . . . .

. . . . .ten mums in coats, talking
    nine babes in prams, squawking
    eight dads their cars parking
    seven dogs on leads barking

    six toddlers all squabbling
    five Grans on bikes wobbling
    four child-minders running
    three bus drivers sunning

    two teenagers dating
    one lollipop man waiting. . . . .

The school is out,
it's half past three
and the first to the school gate
. . . . .is me!

Wes Magee

The Lollipop Lady

When
we come to the
busy street we stand
beside the kerb and wait.
The lady with the lollipop
makes the teatime traffic stop.
When it's our turn to go across
even the hugest lorries pause.
Her lolly's like a magic wand —
cars bicycles and buses stand
and wait until we're over on
the other pavement. Once
we're gone the traffic
all begins to flow
but only

w
h
e
n

s
h
e

s
i
g
n
a
l
s

G
O
!

Pamela Gillilan

Rhinoceros stew

If you want to make a rhinoceros stew
all in the world that you have to do
is skin a rhinoceros, cut it in two
and stew it and stew it and stew it.

When it's stewed so long that you've quite forgot
what it is that's bubbling in the pot
dish it up promptly, serve it hot
and chew it and chew it and chew it

and chew it and chew it and chew it
and chew it and chew it and chew it.

ᴛᴉ ᴡƎHƆ ᗡN∀ ᴛᴉ ᴡƎHƆ ᗡN∀ ᴛᴉ ᴡƎHƆ ᗡN∀

Mildred Luton

30

Gorilla

A giant Gorilla came to tea,
Whoever asked him? It wasn't me.
He came in through the kitchen wall,
It took six chairs to seat him all.
He drank his tea straight from the pot,
And sandwiches – he ate the lot.
He poked the jellies to make them wobble,
Then swallowed them up with just one gobble.
All that remained on the plate was the cake,
There was nothing else for him to take.
When he'd eaten that I showed him the door,
And hoped he'd go now there was no more.
Instead he ate the door as well,
Except for the knocker and the bell.
After that he at last decided to go,
Who invited him? I'd like to know.

Martin Honeysett

In the Kitchen

In the kitchen
After the aimless
Chatter of the plates,
The murmuring of the gas,
The chuckles of the water pipes
And the sharp exchanges
Of the knives, forks and spoons,
Comes the serious quiet
When the sink slowly clears its throat,
And you can hear the occasional rumble
Of the refrigerator's tummy
As it digests the cold.

John Cotton

A Fridge

A fridge is a big white
block of cold
like a snowman
with a door in.

A fridge is a big white
block of cold
like an ice cream
with a light in.

A fridge is a big white
block of cold
like a snowstorm
with milk in.

Martyn Wiley and Ian McMillan

Downhill

I'm rushing
I'm dashing
Through puddles
I'm splashing,
Feet on the handlebars
Hands clinging tight.
I'm gliding
I'm sliding
Hair flying
I'm trying
To keep on the saddle
The bridge is in sight.

I'm singing
Bell ringing
Wind whipping
I'm slipping
About the corner
So fast I could scream!
Still faster!
Disaster!
Brakes failing
I'm sailing
Over the handlebars
Into the stream!

Sheila Simmons

Since Hanna Moved Away

The tyres on my bike are flat.
The sky is grouchy gray.
At least it sure feels like that
Since Hanna moved away.

Chocolate ice cream tastes like
prunes.
December's come to stay.
They've taken back the Mays and
Junes
Since Hanna moved away.

Flowers smell like halibut.
Velvet feels like hay.
Every handsome dog's a mutt
Since Hanna moved away.

Nothing's fun to laugh about.
Nothing's fun to play.
They call me, but I won't come
out
Since Hanna moved away.

Judith Viorst

35

Don't Go Ova Dere

Barry madda tell im
But Barry wouldn' hear,
Barry fada warn im
But Barry didn' care.
"Don' go ova dere, bwoy,
Don' go ova dere."

Barry sista beg im
Barry pull her hair,
Barry brother bet im
"You can't go ova dere."
"I can go ova dere, bwoy,
I can go ova dere."

Barry get a big bag,
Barry climb de gate,
Barry granny call im
But Barry couldn' wait.
Im wan' get ova dere, bwoy.
Before it get too late.

Barry see de plum tree
Im didn' see de bull,
Barry thinkin' bout de plums
"Gwine get dis big bag full".
De bull get up an' shake, bwoy,
An gi de rope a pull.

De rope slip off de pole
But Barry didn' see,
De bull begin to stretch im foot dem
Barry climb de tree,
Barry start fe eat bwoy,
Firs' one, den two, den three.

Barry nearly full de bag
An den im hear a soun'
Barry hol' de plum limb tight
An start fe look aroun'
When im see de bull, bwoy,
Im nearly tumble down.

Night a come, de bull naw move,
From unda de plum tree,
Barry madda wondering
Whey Barry coulda be.
Barry getting tired, bwoy,
Of sittin' in dat tree.

An Barry dis realise
Him neva know before,
Sey de tree did full o' black ants
But now im know fe sure.
For some begin fe bite im, bwoy,
Den more, an more, an more.

De bull lay down fe wait it out,
Barry mek a jump,
De bag o' plum drop out de tree
An Barry hear a thump.
By early de nex' mawnin', bwoy,
Dat bull gwine have a lump.

De plum so frighten dat po' bull
Im start fe run too late,
Im a gallop afta Barry
But Barry jump de gate.
De bull jus' stamp im foot, bwoy,
Im yeye dem full o' hate.

When Barry ketch a im yard,
What a state im in!
Im los' im bag, im clothes mud up,
An mud deh pon im chin.
An whey de black ants bite im
Feba bull-frog skin.

Barry fada spank im.
Im mada sey im sin,
Barry sista scold im
But Barry only grin,
For Barry brother shake im head
An sey, 'Barry, yuh win!'

Valerie Bloom

Sulk

I scuff
  my feet along
And puff
  my lower lip
I sip my milk
  in slurps
And huff
And frown
And stamp around
And tip my chair
  back from the table
Nearly fall down
  but I don't care
I scuff
And puff
And frown
And huff
And stamp
And pout
Till I forget
What it's about.

Felice Holman

38

To Beat Bad Temper

An angry tiger in a cage
Will roar and roar and roar with rage,
And gnash his teeth and lash his tail,
For that's how tigers rant and rail.
I keep my temper in a cage,
I hate it when it roars with rage,
I hate its teeth, I hate its tail,
So when it starts to rant and rail,
I tell my mum, I tell my dad,
I tell them why it's feeling bad,
And then I skip and skip and skip.
And lash my rope just like a whip,
And when I skip because I'm cross,
My temper-tiger knows who's boss,
And when I've skipped and whipped like mad,
My temper-tiger's not so bad.
I have to keep it tame this way,
Or it will eat me up one day.

Cynthia Mitchell

In the Wood

One, two, three, four,
They've begun to count . . .
I race into the wood to hide
Thump down the dry-mud track
Dive off through grass and hazel clumps
Crash between bracken-stalks and snatching brambles
Crouch in a secret hollow,
Wait.

Echoing 'Cooeee's'
As they follow;
Laughter,
Crack of branches
As they call my name,
Call; call again,
Then stop.

Foxgloves rear up all round me
Dragon-necked, with purple tongues;
Fern-fronds lay long hands over me
Stifling with the greenness of their heavy smell;
Swarms of small flies annoy.

The wood falls quiet;
I hear my heart;
Then some minute wild squeaking
Deep in the ocean of the leaves.
Upon the air a thin dynamic hum,
The sound of summer.
No other person in the world but me.

Shiela Simmons

Richard's Brother Speaks

Richard . . .
What's the matter? Why you not smiln' no more?
You wretch, you bruk the window?
Daddy a go peel you 'kin,
'Im a go peel it like how he peel orange.
When Daddy come true dat door
You better run.
You better leave de country!
'Im a-go peel you 'kin.
You bottom a go warm tonight though!
Me goin' cook dinner pon you backside
When 'im done wid you
Richard 'im a come!
Run, bwoy, run!

Desmond Strachan

Stevie

Stevie pelting Ma Rose mango
With his good friend Hicks
Even though his mother tell him
He would get some licks.

Stevie pick up a big boulder
And he aim with zest
What he thought was Julie mango
Was a big jap nest.

The japs start swarming Stevie head
And he start to squeal
His mother said, 'I tired tell you
Who don't hear does feel.'

Odette Thomas

43

Bees

(a poem to read with your youngest brother or sister)

Bees on your fingers,
Bees on your toes,
Bees in your ear-holes
And bees up your nose.

Bees on your tongue-tip,
Bees between your teeth.
Bees, bees on top of bees
And bees underneath.

Bees in your toothpaste,
Bees on your brush,
Bees going Boom Boom!
And bees going Hush.

Bees on your Weetabix,
Bees wearing boots,
Bees dressed in T shirts
And bees in best suits.

Bees up the chimney,
Bees down the drain,
Bees bumping into bees,
Oh not bees again!

Bees in your satchel.
Bees in your bed,
Bees live a buzzy life
Then drop down dead.

John Mole

44

The Tooth Exthpert

My thithter lotht a tooth today,
I with it had been me,
But I've lotht theven anyway,
You probably can thee.
I love the trickth that you can play
Beneath a wobbly tooth;
I think I found one yethterday,
Which may be coming looth.
You thlide your tongue beneath the gap,
It'th jagged, like a thaw,
And if you puth it back and forth
You loothen it thome more.
But, if your tooth ith thtubborn,
And thtill hanging by a thread,
You get some thtring, and make a nooth,
And tie the looth end to a bed . . . .
Then thomeone hath to tickle you,
To make you jump about,
And tho, before you notith it,
The tooth ith pulled right out.

P.ETH.
Don't thwallow it, for goodneth thake,
Jutht keep it thafe and thound,

And then you'll get a fivepenth,
When the tooth fairieth come round.

Susan Stranks

46

Ruth Luce and Bruce Booth

Said little Ruth Luce
to little Bruce Booth:
"Lithen," said Ruth
"I've a little looth tooth!"

Said little Bruce Booth:
"Tho what if you do?
that'th nothing thpethial –
I've a looth tooth too!"

N.M. Bodecker

The Dentist

I love to visit my dentist
and read the comics there,
to see his rows of clackety teeth
and ride in his moving chair.

I love to visit my dentist
and stare at his stripey fish,
to see the pink fizz in the glass
and the fillings on the dish.

I love to visit my dentist
and see his tools all gleam,
but when I need a filling –
well, then I'm *not* so keen!

Judith Nicholls

47

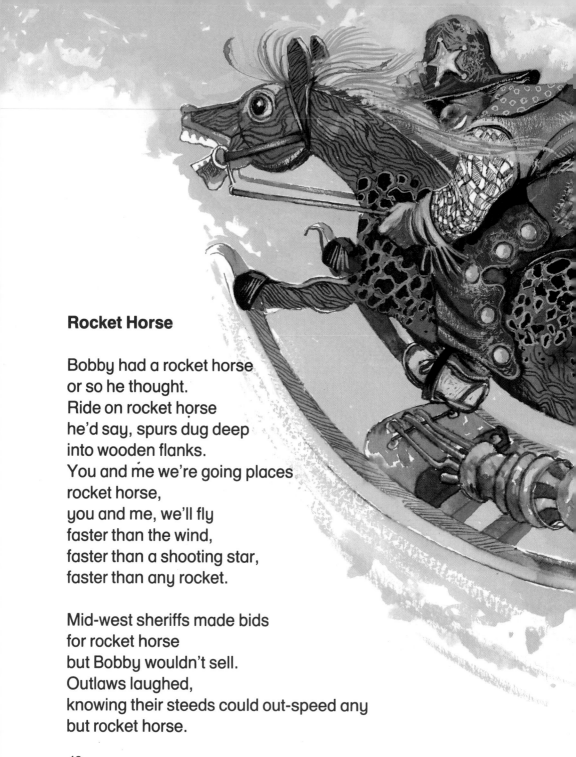

Rocket Horse

Bobby had a rocket horse
or so he thought.
Ride on rocket horse
he'd say, spurs dug deep
into wooden flanks.
You and me we're going places
rocket horse,
you and me, we'll fly
faster than the wind,
faster than a shooting star,
faster than any rocket.

Mid-west sheriffs made bids
for rocket horse
but Bobby wouldn't sell.
Outlaws laughed,
knowing their steeds could out-speed any
but rocket horse.

Some say he's a Wizard
Some say he's a Saint
Some say he eats toads for his tea
So I don't think I'll pay
Him a visit today
For fear he should want to eat me.

Gareth Owen

The Hour when the Witches Fly

When the night is as cold as stone,
When lightning severs the sky,
When your blood is chilled to the bone,
That's the hour when the witches fly.

When the night-owl swoops for the kill,
When there's death in the fox's eye,
When the snake is coiled and still,
That's the hour when the witches fly.

When the nightmares scream in your head,
When your hear a strangled cry,
When you startle awake in your bed,
That's the hour when the witches fly.

When the sweat collects on your brow,
When the minutes tick slowly by,
When you wish it was then not now,
That's the hour when the witches fly.

John Foster

Disbelief

I don't believe in werewolves
    or the mummy from the tomb,
I don't believe in vampires
    in the corner of the room.
I don't believe in lots of things
    for now I'm getting older,
But I *do* believe a skeleton
    just tapped me on the shoulder.

Doug Macleod

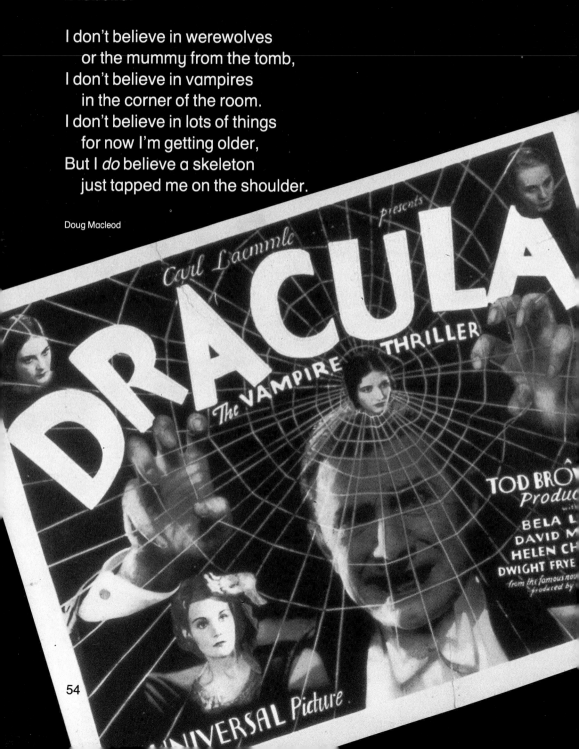

The Ghost in the Garden

The ghost in the garden
Cracks twigs as she treads
Shuffles the leaves
But isn't there
Snaps back the brambles
So they spring against my legs
But isn't there
Draws spiders' webs across my face
Breathes on my cheek
Whispers with bird-breath down by ear
Tosses raindrops down from branches
But isn't there
Splashes the pond
Traces a face in it that isn't mine
Moves shadows underneath the trees
Spreads bindweed out to catch me
Flutters wild wings about my head
Beating into my hair
But when I look
There's only the bend of grass where her running feet
Have smudged the dew,
And there's only the soft sigh
Of her laughter
Trickling
Like moonlight
On wet
Weeds.

Berlie Doherty

Grandpa Bear's Lullaby

The night is long
But fur is deep.
You will be warm
In winter sleep.

The food is gone
But dreams are sweet
And they will be
Your winter meat.

The cave is dark
But dreams are bright
And they will serve
As winter light.

Sleep, my little cubs, sleep.

Jane Yolen

Bedtime

When I go upstairs to bed,
I usually give a loud cough.
This is to scare The Monster off.

When I come to my room,
I usually slam the door right back.
This is to squash The Man in Black
Who sometimes hides there.

Nor do I walk to the bed,
But usually run and jump instead.
This is to stop The Hand –
Which is under there all right –
From grabbing my ankles.

Allan Ahlberg

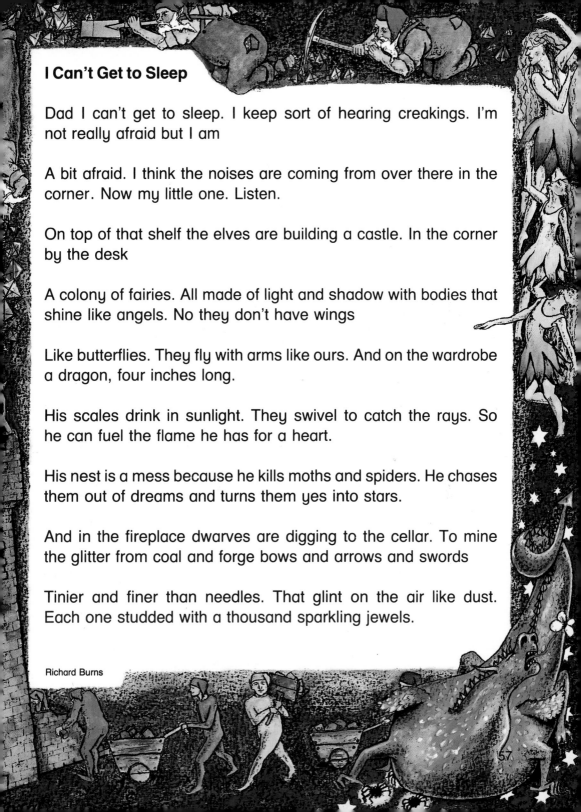

I Can't Get to Sleep

Dad I can't get to sleep. I keep sort of hearing creakings. I'm not really afraid but I am

A bit afraid. I think the noises are coming from over there in the corner. Now my little one. Listen.

On top of that shelf the elves are building a castle. In the corner by the desk

A colony of fairies. All made of light and shadow with bodies that shine like angels. No they don't have wings

Like butterflies. They fly with arms like ours. And on the wardrobe a dragon, four inches long.

His scales drink in sunlight. They swivel to catch the rays. So he can fuel the flame he has for a heart.

His nest is a mess because he kills moths and spiders. He chases them out of dreams and turns them yes into stars.

And in the fireplace dwarves are digging to the cellar. To mine the glitter from coal and forge bows and arrows and swords

Tinier and finer than needles. That glint on the air like dust. Each one studded with a thousand sparkling jewels.

Richard Burns

57

I Often Meet a Monster

I often meet a monster
While deep in sleep at night;
And I confess to some distress.
It gives me quite a fright.
But then again I wonder.
I have this thought, you see.
Do little sleeping monsters scream
Who dream
Of meeting me?

Max Fatchen

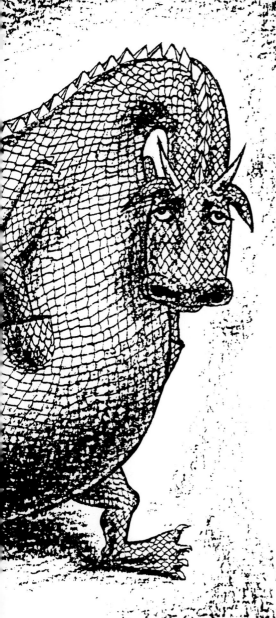

The Lonely Dragon

A dragon is sad
Because everyone thinks
A dragon is fierce and brave,
And roars out flames,
And eats everybody,
Whoever comes near his cave.
But a dragon likes people,
A dragon needs friends,
A dragon is lonely and sad,
If anyone knows
Of a friend for a dragon,
A dragon would be very glad.

Theresa Heine

Feather or Fur

When you watch for
Feather or fur
Feather or fur
Do not stir
Do not stir.

Feather or fur
Come crawling
Creeping
Some come peeping
Some by night
And some by day.
Most come gently
All come softly
Do not scare
A friend away.

When you watch for
Feather or fur
Feather or fur
Do not stir
Do not stir.

John Becker

Waking

My secret way of waking
is like a place
to hide.
I'm very still,
my eyes are shut.
They all think I am sleeping
but
I'm wide awake inside.

They all think I am sleeping
but
I'm wiggling my toes.
I feel sun-fingers
on my cheek.
I hear voices whisper-speak.
I squeeze my eyes
to keep them shut
so they will think I'm sleeping
BUT
I'm really wide awake inside
– and no one knows!

Lilian Moore

61

Oscar the Dog

I'm Oscar the Dog,
I'm my own dog not theirs,
In spite of whatever they think,
So I'll fight and I'll run
And have lots of fun,
And find dirty puddles to drink.

I'm Oscar the Dog
And my breed's Dartmoor Terrier,
And let me tell you for free,
That I bark and I pull,
And I'm never so merrier
Than sniffing and being just me.

I'm Oscar the Dog
And when I am called
I keep them all waiting a while.
Though I go in the end
I like to pretend
I'll run off, 'cause that is my style.

I'm Oscar the Dog
And I'm all for Dog's Lib,
Though my mistress tells people I'm good,
So I growl at her friends
And water her plants
To make sure it's quite understood,

That I'm Oscar the Dog
And when I'm called bad

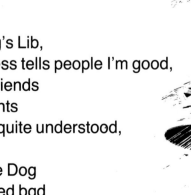

I smile and I wag my small tail,
And as for a smack,
It's like a pat on the back,
I tell you it really can't fail!

I'm Oscar the Dog
And I'm everyone's friend
When there's something to offer or give,
A biscuit or tit bit,
I really don't mind,
After all, a dog's got to live.

John Cotton

Pets

I'm a dog
All tail and bark,
Snapping, yapping
In the park.

I'm a cat
As thin as wire,
Creeping, sleeping
By the fire.

I'm a rabbit
All fluff and ear,
Trapped in a cage
And twitching fear.

John Kitching

My Cat

My cat
got fatter
and fatter.
I didn't know
what was the matter.
Then,
know what she did?
She went into the cupboard
and hid.

She was fat when she went in,
but she came out
thin.
I had a peep.
Know what I saw?
Little kittens
all in a heap
– 1 – 2 – 3 – 4.

My cat's great.

Nigel Gray

Fish

fat
cat
swish
fish

purr
fur
wish
fish

paw
below
dip
flip

mouth
wide
fish
slip
slide
inside

lips
lick

cat
nap

John Cunliffe

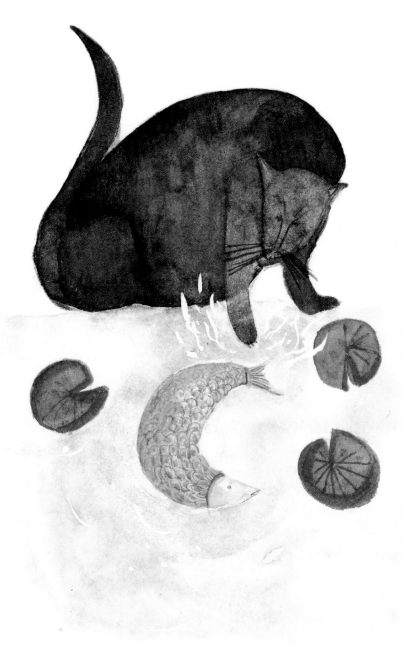

Thank You, Dad, for Everything

Thank you for laying the carpet, dad,
Thank you for showing us how,
But what is that lump in the middle, dad?
And why is it saying mia-ow?

Doug Macleod

Hair, There and Everywhere

My dad who's as bald as a bat
Spilt hair tonic all over the mat.
Now it's grown so much higher
We can't see the fire
And we've searched it in vain for the cat.

Frank Richards

66

Put the Cat Out

Put the cat out father said
Before you go to bed,
But feeling rather naughty
I put father out instead.
"You little rascal let me in"
My angry father cried.
But I quite liked it, as it was
Being on my own inside.
Several months have now gone by
And father's still out there,
Though he seems to have changed,
For his body is now
Covered in masses of hair.
He's even developed a bit of a tail,
Each finger's become a claw,
And in return for bowls of milk
He leaves dead mice at the door.

Martin Honeysett

Giraffe

Giraffe,
Sometimes
You make me laugh,
Way up there
In the skies.

But when
You stoop
To stare at me,
You cut me
Down to size.

John Foster

Turtles

When turtles hide within their shells
There is no way of knowing
Which is front and which is back
And which way which is going.

John Travers Moore

Centipedes

The Centipedes in my garden
   Are such noisy little brutes,
I wish that they'd wear slippers
   Instead of hobnail boots.

Martin Honeysett

I'm a Parrot

I'm a parrot
I live in a cage
I'm nearly always
in a vex-up rage

I used to fly
all light and free
in the luscious
green forest canopy

I'm a parrot
I live in a cage
I'm nearly always
in a vex-up rage

I miss the wind
against my wing
I miss the nut
and the fruit picking

I'm a parrot
I live in a cage
I'm nearly always
in a vex-up rage

I squawk I talk
I curse I swear
I repeat the things
I shouldn't hear

I'm a parrot
I live in a cage
I'm nearly always
in a vex-up rage

So don't come near me
or put out your hand
because I'll pick you
if I can

pickyou
pickyou
if I can

I want to be free
CAN'T YOU UNDERSTAND

Grace Nichols

70

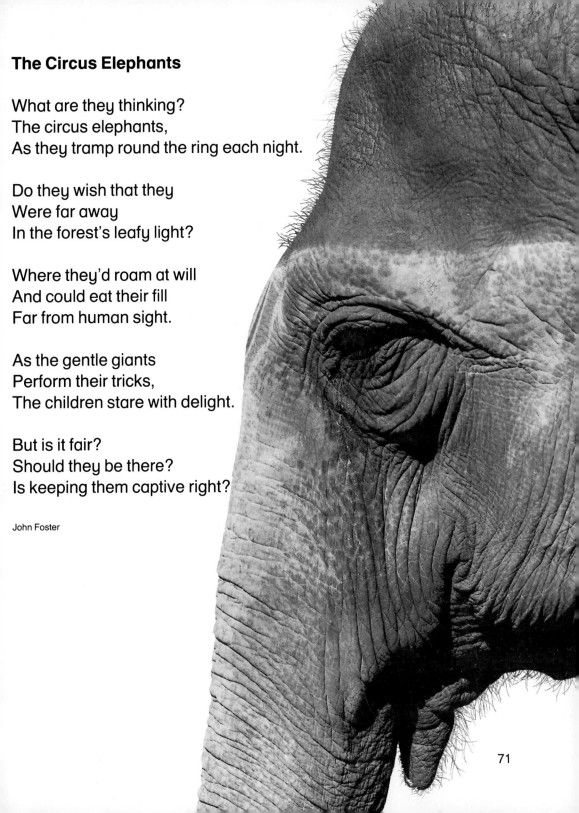

The Circus Elephants

What are they thinking?
The circus elephants,
As they tramp round the ring each night.

Do they wish that they
Were far away
In the forest's leafy light?

Where they'd roam at will
And could eat their fill
Far from human sight.

As the gentle giants
Perform their tricks,
The children stare with delight.

But is it fair?
Should they be there?
Is keeping them captive right?

John Foster

71

Chameleons

Chameleons are seldom seen,
They're red, they're orange, then they're green.
They're one of nature's strangest sights,
Their colours change like traffic lights.

Colin West

Mother Alligator's Advice to her Children

Don't eat too much sweet
You'll spoil your lovely teeth.

Don't touch jelly or treacle
Stick to eating people.

John Agard

The Lion

The lion just adores to eat
A lot of red and tender meat,
And if you ask the lion what
Is much the tenderest of the lot,
He will not say a roast of lamb
Or curried beef or devilled ham

Or crisp pork or corned-beef hash
Or sausages or mutton mash.
Then could it be a big plump hen?
He answers 'No'. What is it, then?
Oh, lion dear, could I not make
You happy with a lovely steak?

Could I entice you from your lair
With rabbit pie or roasted hare?
The lion smiled and shook his head.
He came up very close and said,
'The meat I am about to chew
Is neither steak nor chops. It's you.'

Roald Dahl

75

Hippopotamuses

Hippopotamuses never
Put on boots in rainy weather.
To slosh in mud up to their ears
Brings them great joy and merry tears.
Their pleasure lies in being messed up
They just won't play at being dressed up.
In fact a swamp is heaven plus
If you're a hippopotamus.

Arnold Spilka

The Muddy Puddle

I am sitting
In the middle
Of a rather Muddy
Puddle,
With my bottom
Full of bubbles
And my wellies
Full of Mud,

While my jacket
And my sweater
Go on slowly
Getting wetter
As I very
Slowly settle
To the Bottom
Of the Mud.

And I find that
What a person
With a puddle
Round his middle
Thinks of mostly
In the muddle
Is the Muddi-
Ness of Mud.

Dennis Lee

I saw

I saw an Elephant
Trying to wipe
The sweat on his trunk
While smoking a pipe!

I saw a Camel
Trying to jump
Right over a hill
That was only his hump!

I saw a Horse
As swift as a gale
Trying to catch up
With its own tail!

I saw a Tiger
Trying to wash
Himself in a tub
Of lemon squash!

Harindranath Chattopadhyaya

78

79

Whoosh!

Careering,
and
veering
without
any
steering,
I fly
through the air
in dismay.
With
a skid
and
a roll
I am
out of
control
and
you'd better
keep
out of
my way.
I'm oozily
gliding
and
sliding
and
riding
like
a sledge
on a
slippery
slope
until,
quite unsmiling,
I THUMP
on the
tiling.
How I dread
when I tread
on the
soap.

Max Fatchen

Soap

Soap lives in water
And is hard to catch,
Slipping through your fingers
Especially in the bath.

It hasn't a handle to hold
And can't be fastened with
                           string;
It hasn't a zip to close
Or a cardboard box to go in.

It doesn't answer a whistle
Or come for milk or a biscuit;
It won't go into a kennel
Or curl up and sleep in a
                           basket.

Soap is a square slippery
                           fish:
I wish it would stay in its
                           place
And not always vanish
While I'm washing my face.

Stanley Cook

Slide

I count aloud
as I clang up the steps
to the top of the slide in the park.
The wind is pulling my hair about
and my hands are cold
and my shirt's hanging out
and I've got to go down that glittery slide
that steep and slippery glittery slide
to get to the bottom again. . . .
So . . .
   I close my eyes . . .

                let go . . .

                     and whoosh. . . .

I swoop like a diving plane!
Off with a jump,
back to the steps
and up to the top again!

Sheila Simmons

Places

There are Go-through places
(Arches and doorways).
There are Crawl-under places
(Fence or wall).
But the Climb-up places
(Clear to the tiptops)
Are the very best places of all!

John Travers Moore.

Davy's First Switchback

He clung
to the metal bar, clench-
ing it
TIGHT
as it swung
and wrench-
ed him
left, right
backforwards
sideways and Oh
up up up UP
(will it never touch the top?)
to a sick-
en-
ing
PLUNGE
and an end-
less
drop
drop
dropping
down
a dark pit-
shaft
that's
Davy's stomach.
Then a sudden
lunge
and everything slows, steadies, slides
and glides
to a
STOP.

Raymond Wilson

84

The Playground Monster

It grabbed me
with its tarmac jaws
and then it tried
to bite me.

It grasped me
with its gravelly paws
and then it tried
to fight me.

I live in fear of walking
across its great black back.

I think it knows I'm talking.
It listens at a crack!

I fear its greedy darkness,
the way it seems to need

to reach out when I'm running
and grab me for a feed.

I fear its wrinkled skin
that is warted like a toad

and its grimey darkened skull
that heaves beneath the load.

It grabbed me
with its tarmac jaws
and then it tried
to bite me.
It grasped me
with its gravelly paws
and then it tried
to fight me. . . . . .

Pie Corbett

Sizing Things Up

To a worm that's under me,
I must look very tall.
BUT . . .
To a bird that's up a tree,
I must look very small!

But . . .
If we all sat up a tree
(or maybe on a wall,)
And someone else could see us three,
I'd be biggest of us all!

Ian Larmont

Walls

I like a wall —
a wall to walk on —
a wall to jump off,
a wall to talk on:

It might be big
or it might be small,
as slim as a willow
or a boy-sized wall.

I like a wall
where snails are climbing
slower than slow,
their grey shells shining;

I like a wall
with bricks, and places
to put your toe in
and count your paces.

I like a wall
with flint and grit
and a sun-warmed stone
in the heart of it;

Walls that are smooth
and walls with bumps on,
smothered in moss,
or sharp, with lumps on;

Walls that are narrow
and walls that are wider . . .
walls that are carrying
ant and spider,

Walls that are new
and pink and bold,
walls that are crumbling,
old . . . old. . . .

And I know a wall
with a place to rest in
secret and snug.

It's got a nest in!

Jean Kenward

87

I am the Rain

I am the rain
I like to play games
like sometimes I pretend
I'm going to
        fall
Man that's the time
I don't come at all

Like sometimes
I get these laughing stitches
up my sides
rushing people in
        and out
with the clothesline

I just love
      drip
      dropping
      down
      collars
      and spines

Maybe it's a shame
but it's the only way
I get some fame

Grace Nichols

The Rainbow

The rainbow's like a coloured bridge
that sometimes shines from ridge to ridge.
Today one end is in the sea,
the other's in this field with me.

Iain Crichton-Smith

Think of Tree

Under
the car smell

over
the tar smell

a sweet green and far smell
flows
down the street.

And it says
drifting by,
    'Think of tree.
    Think of sky.
    Think of ripe apples
    and hay, sun-dry.'

Then you know —
not far away
they are cutting grass
in the park today.

Lilian Moore

All Kinds of Trees

on the park
there are trees
with leaves
shaped like hands

others have
silvery bark

some trees grow tall
some trees stay small
and some grow so broad
and so high and so grand
they must see things
that happen
all over the land

Joan Poulson

Sunshine

If I could hold sunshine
I could lighten the dark,
warm up a cold sea
or brighten the park.

I'd scare away dragons,
melt pathways through snow
and when it was raining
I'd make a rainbow.

If I could hold sunshine
what would I do?
I'd grow a big sunflower
and give it to you.

Rose Flint

Making Hay

I watched them making hay today
they tossed the bales round easily
like golden playing-bricks for giants
in a meadow smelling sweetly

Joan Poulson

The Butterfly

The sun is on fire
In the sky
And in its warmth
Flowers open
In the garden
And the butterfly
Flutters by.

Wings widespread,
It stops to feed
At the flowerbed
And on its favourite flower
The butterfly settles
Like two extra petals.

Stanley Cook

Crows

I like to walk
And hear the black crows talk.

I like to lie
And watch crows sail the sky.

I like the crow
That wants the wind to blow:

I like the one
That thinks the wind is fun.

I like to see
Crows spilling from a tree,

And try to find
The top crow left behind.

I like to hear
Crows caw that spring is near.

I like the great
Wild clamour of crow hate

Three farms away
When owls are out by day.

I like the slow
Tired homeward-flying crow;

I like the sight
Of crows for my good night.

David McCord

The Giggle of Wings

Feeling sad one summer's day
because there was no one to play with,
I lay down on our lawn
to watch the sky,
saw bears chasing lions
across the blue plains of afternoon;
as a flock of geese arrowed towards the pond
felt the grass tickle my skin,
and the giggle of their wings
made me grin at heaven.

Frank Flynn

Wings

If I had wings
    I would touch the fingertips of clouds
        and glide on the wind's breath.

If I had wings
    I would taste a chunk of the sun,
        as hot as peppered curry.

If I had wings
    I would listen to the clouds of sheep bleat
        that graze on the blue.

If I had wings
    I would breath deep and sniff
        the scent of raindrops.

If I had wings
    I would gaze at the people
        who cling to the earth.

If I had wings
    I would dream of
        swimming the deserts
          and walking the seas.

Pie Corbett

Balloon Seller

Buy a balloon,
I have heart ones and round ones,
pink ones and blue ones,
and merry-go-round ones.
Balloons that are diamond shaped,
triangles too,
they dance with the clouds
in the soft springtime blue.

Theresa Heine

Seaside

I like the seaside.
I like the sea –
I like the green wave
over me!
Slip and slither
and flow and flop. . . .
it never seems
to rest, or stop.
It bears the great ships
on its track
and takes them forward
and brings them back;
and in its deepest
depths, I know
luminous, bright skinned
fishes go.

The bit I paddle in's
small and sweet:
it cools my ankles
and smooths my feet.
And yet, they say
there's a great deal more,
and someone paddles
on a different shore –
a different beach
with different things,
and birds with scarlet
on their wings. . . . . .
I guess, wherever
it might be,
I'd like the seaside.
I'd like the sea.

Jean Kenward

The Sea

Deep glass-green seas
chew rocks
with their green-glass jaws.
But little waves
creep in
and nibble softly at the sand.

Lilith Norman

Stony

We found this secret beach
Of sea-smooth stones last year:
What fun we had here!
We flung them out to sea at first
Over the running tide,
Your lazy throws
Always the winners
No matter how hard I tried.
Then we bombed blobs
Of seaweed
With nearly fist-sized stones:
At hits and near-misses
Gave cheers or groans,
Till, leaning against two boulders,
Arms round each other's shoulders
We listened to shifting stones
In the tug and suck of the sea;
Last year, you and me.

This year, remembering,
I walked the beach alone
And everything was cold
And grey as stone.

Eric Finney

Jetsam

Foaming wave. . .aftershave
Plastic comb, brittle bone
Bottle top, building block
Wooden spar, plastic car
Thermos top, can of pop
Salt-stained shoe, tin of glue
Tennis racket, empty packet
Car tyre, coil of wire
Pram wheel, rubber seal
Tar-blacked stone, fir cone
Rusty lid, twisted grid
Chipboard, orange cord
Empty and faded
Bottle of bleach
Almost forgetten
On a winter beach.

Nigel Cox

103

Footprints

I left my footprints on the sand
    and watched them follow me,
For every place that I had gone
    I saw them by the sea.
But when the tide came in, it washed
    my footprints all away
And left no trace of them upon
    the sand I trod today.

John Travers Moore

Sand

Sand in your fingernails
Sand between your toes
Sand in your earholes
Sand up your nose!

Sand in your sandwiches
Sand on your bananas
Sand in your bed at night
Sand in your pyjamas!

Sand in your sandals
Sand in your hair
Sand in your trousers
Sand everywhere!

John Foster

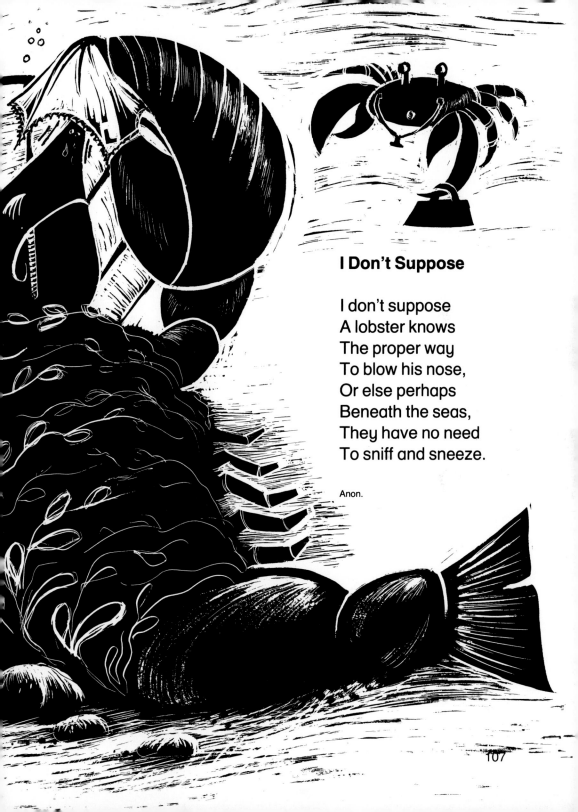

I Don't Suppose

I don't suppose
A lobster knows
The proper way
To blow his nose,
Or else perhaps
Beneath the seas,
They have no need
To sniff and sneeze.

Anon.

Excuses

I only took it off
For a minute and a bird
Flew away with it.
I know it sounds absurd.

I only put it down
While I tied my shoelace
And a squirrel popped off with it.
At such a pace!

I only laid it on the grass
While we were playing and a cow
Munched it. I wonder
Where it is now.

I only tucked it under my arm
And a horse came up behind me –
Took it in his big teeth.
Please don't remind me

That once I had two pairs
Of woolly gloves (that makes four
I've lost) and it's cold now, nearly
Christmas. Can we buy some more?

Pamela Gillilan

Dufflecoat

It has four toggles made of wood,
it's warm and snug inside the hood –
but I find it very diffle-dufflecult
to do up my navy fiddle-fuddlecoat.

John Rice

109

Letters to Santa

Dere Farther Crismus pleas cum soon
and bring me a nise big red balloon.

                I luv you.   Andrew (aged 2)

Dear Santa, I'm writing to say that I'd like
a jigsaw, some roller-boots and a bike.
                And a desk if you can.   From Anne

Dear Father Christmas, would you please not present
me with slippers – or knickers? I'd rather have scent.
                I'm not being funny.   Love, Mummy

Memo to F.C. Remember – no ties!
Or no whisky for you and no warm mince-pies.
                Good lad!   Dad

Just a note to say I'd appreciate some
Tobacco, a new scarf and a bottle of rum.
                Ta.   Grandpa

Dear Santa Claus, here is a letter
to say one bone would be nice, but two would be better.
                Don't think I'm a hog.   Fred (the dog)

P.S.   Please tell your reindeer
            I'm sorry I barked at them last year.

Jacqueline Brown

High in the Heaven

High in the Heaven
A gold star burns
Lighting our way
As the great world turns.

Silver the frost
It shines on the stem.
As we now journey
To Bethlehem.

White is the ice
At our feet as we tread,
Pointing a path
To the manger-bed

Charles Causley

Christmas Star

There rose a star of burnished gold,
It moved with purpose through the sky,
It carried tidings yet untold,
And watchers gazed as it passed by,
Through mists of day and shadowed night,
It filled the sky with burning light.

Theresa Heine

Christmas Story

Shepherds, wakeful, weary,
On bare hillsides stony,
In the midnight clearly
Hear the angels' story.

Star, jewel-bright, lovely,
Above a stable lowly,
Wherein a maiden, Mary,
Tends a baby gently.

Wise men, rich and mighty,
To Bethlehem ride slowly
To offer presents costly,
Honour the birth of a baby.

In the warm manger, safely,
Christ, the child, sleeps soundly –
To all the poor and lonely
God's gift once only.

Jacqueline Brown

113

The Sky is Black Tonight

The sky is black tonight;
Coal-black, crow-black.
But in that black
Is the white-bright light
Of a star.

That star has a gift tonight:
A birth-gift, for-all-the-earth gift.
For in that star
Is a fly-by-night:
Is a bird!

That bird has a song tonight:
A love-song, high-above-song.
And in that song
Is the silver tongue
Of a bell.

That bell has a wish tonight;
A bell-wish, a well-wish.
And the wish
In the bell
In the song
In the bird
In the star
In the black
In the sky
Is Peace.
Is Peace.
Is Peace.

Berlie Doherty

Snow

Feathery soft and quiet the snow;
It covers the road
   and the walk
   and the rooftops
   and whispers to the world:
          Shhh!

Margaret R. Moore

Heather by Name

The snow covers everything:
The evergreen turns white,
The climbing ivy freezes,
Its stalk encased in ice.
Snow everywhere.
Everywhere snow.

But look:
Heather pushed through the white,
Through the snow.
A cluster of colour.

The question is:
What was she doing there anyway,
Under the snow?

That's easy to answer.
She was
Heather by name,
Heather by nature.
A cluster of colour.

Alan Bold

In Winter

Where does it come from?
Where does it go
hazily drifting
snow on snow,
out of the distance
out of the sky,
further than everything –
high on high?

Is it a goose
that sits up there,
dropping her feathers down
everywhere?
Is it a gander
white and fat?
What is he thinking of?
What is he at?

Why does a snowflake
vanish when
I taste it on my tongue?
And then,
why does it grow
so great and tall
when I roll and roll it
in a ball?

Why is it cold? Why is it wet?
Why do we wait so long
to get
snowflakes
out of the far-off sky –
further than everything,
high on high?

Jean Kenward

Icicle Joe

I made a snowman:
Icicle Joe.
The moon shone round him
high and low. . . .
the moon shone round him
sides and back –
it gave him a shadow,
purple black.

I made a snowman
white and plump;
a nose he had
like a sugar lump.
The sun shone round him. . . .
One bright day
he slumped a little
and he went away.

Vanishing softly
bit by bit
like a lollipop does
when you suck at it,
only a puddle
stayed to show
where I had built him –
Icicle Joe.

Jean Kenward

Snowy Day In the Park

Across the park
the footprints go
criss-crossing crazily
over the snow. . . .

Here a dog has scampered,
here a child has run,
here a mouse on tiny feet
has scuttled in the frosty grass
now sparkling in the sun.

Across the clean white page of the park
the footprints are there to be read,
and we're leaving a message for somebody else
in the wandering patterns we tread.

Shiela Simmons

Almost Spring

One day in March
when the mud oozes,
rugs appear on windowsills
lolling like dusty tongues;
carts sell daffodils –
and the wind, like a paintbrush,
smacks my cheek freshly.

I take off my coat
and shoes, play
in the sun, sweat.
But in the shivery shade
It's not Spring, yet.

Judith Thurman

Breaking Through

Forks
of warm rain
loosen the ice
on the pond.

Morning
turns in the keyhole.
The dark gives,
it opens.

My seed
is growing.
A little shoot
has pushed through
the hard shell.

Judith Thurman

The Tree Man

The Tree Man
groans
The Tree Man
creaks
The cold wind blows
The Tree Man
speaks
Can You hear me
The Tree Man
Says
And the cold wind answers
Yes, yes, yes.

The Tree Man
rises
The Tree Man
bends
His voice through the earth
The Tree Man
Sends
Do the people know
The Tree Man
cries
Who knows?
Says the owl
And the cold wind
Sighs.

Clive Riche

Ways of the Winds

the wind from the west
is a gentle wind
a wind of smiles
a wind of soft stroking

the wind from the east
is a cruel wind
a wind of scowls
a wind of sly chillness

the wind from the north
is a harsh wind
a wind of force
a wind of cold boldness

the wind from the south
is a friendly wind
a wind of laughter
a wind of warm kindness

Joan Poulson

The Tree and the Pool

'I don't want my leaves to drop,' said the tree.
'I don't want to freeze,' said the pool.
'I don't want to smile,' said the sombre man.
'Or ever to cry,' said the Fool.

'I don't want to open,' said the bud,
'I don't want to end,' said the night.
'I don't want to rise,' said the neap-tide,
'Or ever to fall,' said the kite.

They wished and they murmured and whispered,
They said that to change was a crime,
Then a voice from nowhere answered,
'You must do what I say,' said Time.

Brian Patten

Index of first lines

Acknowledgements

The following poems are being published for the first time in this anthology and appear by permission of the author unless otherwise stated:
Valerie Bloom: *Don't Go Ova Dere* © 1987 Valerie Bloom. Alan Bold: *Heather by Name* © 1987 Alan Bold. Jacqueline Brown: *Letters to Santa; Christmas Story:* both © 1987 Jacqueline Brown. Richard Burns: *I Can't Get to Sleep* © 1987 Richard Burns. Stanley Cook: *Soap; The Butterfly* © 1987 Stanley Cook. Pie Corbett: *The Playground Monster; Wings;* both © 1987 Pie Corbett. John Cotton: *In the Kitchen; Oscar the Dog;* both © 1987 John Cotton. Nigel Cox: *Jetsam* © 1987 Nigel Cox. John Cunliffe: *Fish* © 1987 John Cunliffe. Berlie Doherty: *Dad; My Sparrow Gran; Grandpa; The Ghost in the Garden; The Sky is Black Tonight;* all © 1987 Berlie Doherty. Max Fatchen: *Whoosh!* © 1987 Max Fatchen. Eric Finney: *Stony* © 1987 Eric Finney. Rose Flint: *Sunshine* © 1987 Rose Flint. Frank Flynn: *The Giggle of Wings* © 1987 Frank Flynn. John Foster: *The Hour when the Witches Fly; The Circus Elephants; Giraffe; Sand;* all © 1987 John Foster. Pamela Gillilan: *Ticklish; The Lollipop Lady; Excuses;* all © 1987 Pamela Gillilan. Nigel Gray: *My Cat* © Nigel Gray. Gregory Harrison: *Grandpa is very old* © 1987 Gregory Harrison. Theresa Heine: *Friends; Enemies; The Lonely Dragon; Balloon Seller; Christmas Star;* all © 1987 Theresa Heine. Julie Holder: *Where Did the Baby Go?* © 1987 Julie Holder. Martin Honeysett: *Put the Cat Out* © 1987 Martin Honeysett. Jean Kenward: *Walls; Seaside; In winter; Icicle Joe;* all © 1987 Jean Kenward. John Kitching: *Pets* © 1987 John Kitching. Ian Larmont: *Sizing Things Up;* © 1987 Ian Larmont. Wes Magee: *Teacher, Teacher; Down by the School Gate;* both © 1987 Wes Magee. Ian McMillan and Martin Wiley: *Fridge* © 1987 Ian McMillan and Martin Wiley. John Mole: *Bees* © 1987 John Mole. Brian Moses: *Rocket Horse* © 1987 Brian Moses. Grace Nichols: *I am the Rain* © 1987 Grace Nichols. Judith Nicholls: *Sister; My Dad; Storytime; The Dentist;* all © Judith Nicholls. Joan Poulson: *What is it?; All Kinds of Trees; Making Hay; Ways of the Wind;* all © Joan Poulson. John Rice: *Dufflecoat* © 1987 John Rice. Clive Riche: *The Tree Man* © 1987 Clive Riche. Sheila Simmons: *Downhill; In the Wood; Slide; Snowy Day in the Park;* all © 1987 Sheila Simmons. Iain Crichton-Smith: *The Rainbow* © 1987 Iain Crichton-Smith. Raymond Wilson: *Davy's First Switchback* © 1987 Raymond Wilson.

The cover is by Chris Swee. Photographed by Tessa Wilkinson.

The illustrations are by Michael A.E. Beach, Virginia Fitzgerald, Rachel B. Stevens, Jacquelin Stevenson, Carol S. Wright.

The publishers would like to thank the following for permission to reproduce photographs:
The J. Allan Cash Photolibrary p.40, p.84, p.90/1, p.121; Aquarius Photo Library, London p.10; John Birdsall Photography p.14, p.27; Bruce Coleman Limited p.60/1, p.100/1, p.101; Robert Harding Picture Library p.70; The Kobal Collection p.54; Oxford Scientific Films Picture Library p.71, p.72/3; David Richardson p.81.

We are grateful for permission to include the following previously published material in this anthology:

John Agard: 'Mother Alligator's Advice to her children' from *I Din Do Nuttin* by John Agard, illustrated by Susanna Gretz. Reprinted by permission of the Bodley Head. Allan Ahlberg: 'Emma Hackett's Newsbook' and 'Bedtime' from *Please, Mrs Butler* (Kestrel Books, 1983). Copyright © 1983 by Allan Ahlberg. Reprinted by permission of Penguin Books Ltd. Dorothy Aldis: 'Everybody Says', reprinted from *Everything and Anything*, copyright 1925–1927, copyright renewed 1953–1955 by Dorothy Aldis, by permission of G.P. Putnam & Sons. John Becker: 'Feather or Fur', originally published in *New Feathers for the Old Goose* by John Becker. © John Becker. N.M. Bodecker: 'Ruth Luce and Bruce Booth' from *Snowman Sniffles* (A Margaret K. McElderry Book) copyright © 1983 N.M. Bodecker. Reprinted by permission of Faber & Faber Ltd., and Atheneum Publishers Inc., a division of Macmillan, Inc. Charles Causley: 'High in the Heaven' from *The Gift of the Lamb*. Reprinted by permission of Robson Books Ltd. Harindranath Chattopadhyaya: 'I Saw' from *What I Saw*. Courtesy IBH Publishing Co., Bombay. John Ciardi: 'I Wish I Could Meet the Man that Knows' from *I Met a Man*. Copyright © 1961 by John Ciardi. Reprinted by permission of Houghton Mifflin Company. John Cotton: 'In the kitchen', © John Cotton 1985, from *The Crystal Zoo: poems* by John Cotton, L.J. Anderson and V.A. Fanthorpe (1985). Reprinted by permission of Oxford University Press. Roald Dahl: 'The Lion' from *Dirty Beasts* by Roald Dahl, © 1984 by Roald Dahl, illustrated by Quentin Blake. Copyright © 1984 by Roald Dahl. Reprinted by permission of Jonathan Cape Ltd., and Farrar, Straus & Giroux, Inc. Berlie Doherty: 'The Sky is Black Tonight', © 1983, first published as part of a play entitled *The White Bird of Peace*. Reprinted by permission of the author. Max Fatchen: 'I often meet a monster...' from *Wry Rhymes for Troublesome Times* (Kestrel Books, 1983). Copyright © 1983 by Max Fatchen. Reprinted by permission of John Johnson Ltd., and Penguin Books Ltd. Nigel Gray: 'My Cat', © 1975 Nigel Gray. Reprinted by permission of the author. Felice Holman: 'Sulk' from *I Hear You Smiling and Other Poems* (Charles Scribner & Sons, 1973). Reprinted by permission of the author. Martin Honeysett: 'Gorilla' and 'Centipedes' from *Animal Nonsense Rhymes*. Reprinted by permission of Methuen Children's Books. Evan Jones: 'The Duppies' from *Tales of the Caribbean, Witches and Duppies*. Reprinted by permission of Ginn and Company Ltd. Dennis Lee: 'The Muddy Puddle' from *Garbage Delight*, © Dennis Lee 1977. Reprinted by permission of Macmillan of Canada, A Division of Canada Publishing Corporation. Mildred Luton: 'Rhinoceros Stew', © Mildred Luton. Doug Macleod: 'Thank you Dad, for Everything' from *The Fed Up Family Album*; and 'Disbelief' from the *Puffin*